we dare be brave

African American moms and the emotional journey of raising children with disabilities

Salina Miller, AA; Patricia Parker, BA; &
Charisse N. Montgomery, MA, MEd, GPAC

Black & Blue Publishing, LLC • Euclid, Ohio

First Edition: December 2020
Printed in the United States of America
ISBN: 978-1-7333827-6-2

Contact the publisher at supersafekidsbooks@gmail.com.

Cover design by Black & Blue Publishing, LLC
Cover art graphic elements from Shutterstock.com

Touched by an Angel

We, unaccustomed to courage
exiles from delight
live coiled in shells of loneliness
until love leaves its high holy temple
and comes into our sight
to liberate us into life.

Love arrives
and in its train come ecstasies
old memories of pleasure
ancient histories of pain.
Yet if we are bold,
love strikes away the chains of fear
from our souls.

We are weaned from our timidity
In the flush of love's light
we dare be brave
And suddenly we see
that love costs all we are
and will ever be.
Yet it is only love
which sets us free.

DR. MAYA ANGELOU

Contents

Acknowledgements

Salina Miller, AA

I want to acknowledge God first, for bringing together this trinity of amazing women to co-author *We Dare Be Brave*. Patricia Parker and Nikki Montgomery, thank you for your words of wisdom and guidance on this project. I could not have chosen two better women to write my first book with. I am grateful that this book will encourage women of color who are parents of individuals with disabilities.

I want to thank my husband, Robert Miller, for stepping up to raise a child with a disability. He never once shied away from it, loving and caring for Elijah as though he was his own. Thank you for supporting me while I pursue God's purpose for our lives.

Thank you to my boys, Eric and Elijah, who have helped to mold and shape me into the mother and woman that I am today. Elijah, the stories in this book would not be possible without you. Our journey together has been one rollercoaster ride, but the bond we have built can never be broken. Boys, I love you.

This icon appears at the beginning of chapters written by Salina Miller.

• • • • •

Patricia Parker, BA

Whatever God has called you to do, He promises to send the needed resources to accomplish that task. Writing *We Dare Be Brave* in collaboration with Charisse N. Montgomery and Salina Miller has been one of my greatest and most rewarding accomplishments in serving the families of individuals with disabilities. God graced me with the gifts and talents of these two women who are committed to serving families and the community. I celebrate what God has been able to accomplish through this collaboration. I celebrate our connections as sisters in the Lord, as parents of an individual with disabilities, and in our passion for serving individuals with disabilities and their families. *We Dare Be Brave* is the written example of how three African American women can combine information, raw emotions, and experiences sprinkled with passion and love, to unite in serving families within the disabilities community. It's been a privilege and sheer joy, ladies, to have shared this platform with you.

Also, a special thank you to my son Justin, who is always supportive in whatever I do. You have always made me feel I can do anything, and I always remind you that we both can in Christ Jesus. Finally, to my son Matthew, my gift from God, thank you for being who you are, for in doing so you have enriched my life, surrounded me with unconditional love and given me passion and purpose in my life.

This icon appears at the beginning of chapters written by Patricia Parker.

• • • • •

Charisse (Nikki) Montgomery, MA, MEd, GPAC

I thank my family for their ongoing support and encouragement. My late sister, Chavon, and my son, Richie, are the heartbeat of my work to support people with disabilities and their families and caregivers. I thank my wonderful husband for his brilliance, support and endless patience, for listening to my constant brainstorms, and for always supporting my sense of purpose. Iron sharpens iron. ∞

Bringing this project to life had been on my to-do list for years. It merges my love and study of African American women's poetry with my experience of parenting and commitment to advocacy. I am so thankful to my co-authors, Salina and Pat, for their trust and enthusiasm, and especially for their wisdom. These amazing mothers are part of the community of moms I have had the privilege to meet on this journey – moms who raise their children with grace, resilience and pride. I am so grateful to be part of this community, and so proud to call these women my friends and co-authors. Above all, I am grateful for life. Every breath offers us an opportunity to live more fully, love more deeply and walk in our purpose, and I am grateful to the Universe for this gift.

This icon appears at the beginning of chapters written by Charisse (Nikki) Montgomery.

References

Angelou, Maya. "Touched by an Angel." Poem. Accessed online on 2/3/2017: https://cpoem.sunygeneseoenglish.org/2017/01/29/touched-by-an-angel-by-maya-angelou/

Bronfenbrenner, U. (1994). Ecological models of human development. In T. Husen & T. N. Postlethwaite (Eds.), International encyclopedia of education (2nd ed., Vol. 3, pp. 1643–1647). Oxford, UK: Pergamon Press.

Hofer, Barbara & Pintrich, Paul. (1997). The Development of Epistemological Theories: Beliefs About Knowledge and Knowing and Their Relation to Learning. Review of Educational Research. 67. 10.3102/00346543067001088.

Hogan, Dennis P. Family Consequences of Children's Disabilities. New York: Russell Sage Foundation, 2012. Google Book Search. Web. 16 Jan 2015.

John N. Constantino, Anna M. Abbacchi, Celine Saulnier, Cheryl Klaiman, David S. Mandell, Yi Zhang, Zoe Hawks, Julianna Bates, Ami Klin, Paul Shattuck, Sophie Molholm, Robert Fitzgerald, Anne Roux, Jennifer K. Lowe, Daniel H. Geschwind.

Timing of the Diagnosis of Autism in African American Children. Pediatrics Sep 2020, 146 (3) e20193629; DOI: 10.1542/peds.2019-3629

Introduction

Parents who are raising children with disabilities get lots of advice, but most of that advice is about how to do things – how to fill out forms, how to understand an Individualized Education Program (IEP), how to apply for grants. That practical knowledge is helpful, and you can find it easily these days. What we don't often see are tools that help us process and understand the emotions we deal with as parents. We can experience lots of emotions in a day – or even an hour. Our state of mind and the state of our emotions guide how we parent our children; mastering our emotions determines whether we just survive or whether we thrive. The more balanced and aware we are, the more we can focus on what really matters for our children and families.

We Dare Be Brave is the collaboration of three moms who have over 60 years of collective experience with disabilities and advocacy. The authors were inspired by their own experiences, and the words of Dr. Maya Angelou, to share stories of emotional challenge and success, in hopes that you will be empowered, equipped, and inspired to think bigger about your role as the parent of a child with disabilities. There are so many parts of the parenting journey that can be scary and difficult, but you can be confident, skilled, and prepared to fulfill your role when you have a clear vision of the future. There are many, many joys to be found on this path.

There is no shame in feeling emotion; to feel is human. No matter where you are in your parenting journey – from a new diagnosis for an infant or toddler to parenting an adult with disabilities – you will identify with the emotions we all experience and discuss in this book. We can find success as we learn and understand ourselves better. That foundation equips us to meet our children's needs by being well, being intentional and being brave.

PART I
Looking for Meaning in the Journey

We, unaccustomed to courage
exiles from delight
live coiled in shells of loneliness
until love leaves its high holy temple
and comes into our sight
to liberate us into life.

First stanza of "Touched by An Angel"
by Dr. Maya Angelou

Chapter 1
Loneliness

THE EMOTION

Loneliness is a deep sense of sadness because we feel alone. There are many ways we can feel alone as parents. If you are a single parent or don't have family support, that sense of being alone can be very real. Or you might have a partner who is not very involved, leaving you to navigate challenges on your own. You might have many people around you who care, but they see things differently or disagree with your decisions. At the heart of loneliness is the feeling that no one understands the journey we are on, and that no one can really be a support if they don't understand our experience.

The loneliness we feel as we raise our children goes beyond what happens at home and extends into the communities we live in. Our children often have whole systems stacked against them, from late diagnosis of autism to health inequities to the school-to-prison pipeline, just to name a few. Feeling like we have to fight these systems alone is a tremendous workload.

When we go into spaces where there are no other families of color, it leaves us feeling isolated and wondering whether we can find true partnership from people who don't fully understand our experiences. The agencies, healthcare settings and services we use make us feel less safe when there's no representation of families like ours, no faces that look like ours. Sometimes professionals communicate with us in ways that show ignorance of our lives and values. These kinds of encounters add layers to the loneliness we experience as parents.

We deal with bias and overt racism in places that are supposed to feel safe, and many times our voices are silenced by people who think they know more than we do about our needs and challenges. In my experience as a caregiver, healthcare and education professionals have stereotyped me and my family, shown me their biases, and even shut me out of the decision making process for my child. There's nothing lonelier than sitting in a doctor's appointment and feeling powerless, as the doctor makes judgements and decisions based on assumptions. This is another form of isolation and loneliness we might encounter on the parenting journey.

The early part of my journey as a parent was filled with that deep sense of loneliness. My son is medically complex, and at two months old, he had a tracheostomy, a ventilator and a feeding tube, plus speech therapy, occupational therapy, physical therapy and lots of medical specialists. I was terrified that any mistake I made in caring for him could shorten his life. By the time he came home at four months old, I was feeling completely overwhelmed by the complexity of his care.

I felt isolated because we spent most of our time at home back then, to protect our son's fragile body from illness. The first two years were very much like the stay-at-home orders we all lived through with the COVID pandemic. My husband and I were feeling less connected at the time, as we each reset our vision of what our life would look like with our medically complex child. We were communicating from a place of frustration, which placed even more pressure on a stressful situation.

Even though we had in-home nurses, they could be unreliable, and sometimes they didn't have the skills and experience we expected them to have in order to care for our son's complex needs. I didn't know any other families with children as complex as mine. There was nowhere I could take my son without people staring at all his medical equipment or giving me looks of pity. I felt alone.

THE CHALLENGES

Unlike many other parents I have met, I actually knew someone who had a child with the same rare condition my child had – my mother. My younger sister, Chavon, was born in 1985 and was identified as having a disability at birth. While she was less medically complex than our son, Chavon's medical issues made me familiar with the challenges. Despite having a mother who'd had a child with the same diagnosis, there were big differences in the way we approached raising a child with a disability. When my sister was born, my mom turned to her faith through healers and prophets who told her my sister's disability would disappear one day, miraculously.

I understood my mom's need to believe in healing, but I also saw how staying focused on the miracle of healing can make you forget about all the little miracles happening every day. It's understandable why parents want to believe in a time when their child will not experience the difficulties that come from being disabled in a world that is not disability friendly. But it's important to know that with or without healing, your child's life is a miracle in itself. It's important for our children to feel valued as they are and not feel as if their parents are wishing and waiting for them to be something different. Disability is not a curse, not a problem to be fixed. It's the way our children were created, **with** purpose and **on** purpose.

As a side note here, our children have a purpose, but we have to be careful not to exploit them by holding them up for others to use for inspiration. That line can be hard to balance. The adult disabilities community uses the term "disability porn" to describe the way society uses people with disabilities to feel better about their own lives. "My life might not be great, but at least I'm better off than that disabled child" is a damaging message that assumes life with a disability is filled with tragedy. As we navigate helping our children find their purpose, we have to take care not to contribute to the pity and exploitation many people with disabilities deal with daily.

By the time my son was born, I had seen my sister thrive, beat many odds and live proudly and productively as a disabled person. I wanted my son to do the same. For me, disability was a biological variation—like brown eyes or dimples—not a condition to be corrected. I didn't pray for miracles or healing; I prayed for his life—he was so fragile at birth that we weren't sure he'd survive. I also prayed that as his mother, I would be able to help him live his best life—*with* his disability. I believed he was perfect as he was and that his life had meaning. I needed ways to focus on his strengths and raise him in a way that would allow him to reach his potential.

There is so much value in focusing on, and being grateful for, the daily miracles. Most parents feel joy the first time their child eats with a spoon, crawls, or says their first word. After a while though, the excitement of those moments goes away. By the time a child is five or six, eating, crawling and talking aren't seen as special anymore. But the parents of children with disabilities get to experience these miracles on an extended timeline. I'm still excited when my nine-year-old touches a new texture or tastes a new food. I still get to feel those joys with every new milestone.

Having a sister with a disability helped me as I tried to figure out what kind of parent to be for my son. I knew my sister understood what his journey would be like, and I was counting on her help to make sure he grew up feeling valued and loved. Her experience of being raised in our family made her fearless, but she also felt that her disability was treated as a burden at times. I wanted to be sure that I didn't repeat this mistake with my son, and I was depending on my sister to be my teacher.

Being the sibling of a person with a disability helped me to understand the potential of all people, regardless of ability. Chavon was a bright child – a little bit of a know-it-all – and her determination was apparent even when she was little. Always the ringleader, she could get our other siblings to do almost anything, as she sat innocently in her wheelchair and directed their misbehavior. No one in our family was surprised when she completed high school near the top of her class and earned a record number of college scholarships. She finished her bachelor's in Bioinformatics and started a PhD in Bioengineering at Johns Hopkins, traveling all over the country to share her research and learn from others. Overachieving was her habit, and she was unapologetically brilliant.

When Chavon passed away suddenly in 2012, just 10 months after the birth of my son, the loss was enormous. Not only had I lost a baby sister I talked to for many hours every week, I had also lost the person I thought would become a mentor and guide as I raised my child with a disability. The feelings of loneliness I felt after my sister's passing were deep, and these emotions were happening alongside my feelings of being overwhelmed and isolated. The pressure of all of this showed up in my daily life. I was stressed out, short tempered, and exhausted. I was also clinically depressed.

REACHING OUT FOR SOLUTIONS

I was buckling under the pressure of all the change in my life over a short period of time. I eventually began talking to my doctor about my stress. I was hesitant because I didn't want to seem like I resented my son or couldn't handle the challenges. I was grieving in more ways than one; even though I had a husband and family members who were supportive, I felt like the responsibility was all on my shoulders. I needed medication and therapy to help me through those difficult times. But as I healed, I began to see things more clearly and find ways to connect and step out of my isolation.

When our son was a year old, we started attending a therapeutic play group hosted by our local Early Intervention provider. At this play group, I met other mothers who had children with disabilities and delays. I felt less alone; my child had a ventilator and tracheostomy, but no one stared or gave us looks of pity there. I felt connected to their excitement when their children tried a new food at snack time or rolled over on a gym mat during play time. For the first time in my parenting journey, I felt connection.

Overcoming loneliness is about finding where we fit in — finding "our people." If you're fortunate enough to have that sense of community from the start, consider yourself blessed. Many times, we have to seek out our people and create new communities to meet that need for ourselves and for others.

From that first experience with other parents, I was asked to join our local pediatric hospital's family council. The council allowed me to work with other parents who had spent lots of time in the hospital with their medically fragile children. I met great friends and role models, most of whom I still have relationships with today. Our council worked to make the hospital experience better for all families, and we each had a mutual passion for that work, but our bond grew beyond working on hospital projects. We celebrated our children's successes together, supported one another through medical procedures, and helped one another navigate the complexities of healthcare. We became a community, which is exactly what I needed.

I had found a way to use the knowledge I had gained through parenting, and it felt good to give back in that way. I also learned a lot about how the healthcare system works, which has allowed me to help many other families over the years.

I have served on multiple patient and family councils and extended my advocacy in healthcare. I serve on the Board of

Directors at my son's hospital, and I have worked on issues like safety, hospital quality and health equity with partners from around the world. I have a sense of belonging now — I know my experiences matter. I don't feel a sense of loneliness at all anymore because I know my experiences are part of a bigger picture. There are problems to solve, and I feel like I am working within my purpose as I lend my voice to solving those problems.

> *We became a community, which was exactly what I needed.*

Over the years, my son – who uses a wheelchair because of a genetic muscle condition and who is also on the autism spectrum – has participated in many activities that helped us feel like part of a community. He has played adaptive baseball and experienced adaptive dance, kayaking, biking and skateboarding; he has served as a spokesperson and advocated for children's health on Capitol Hill; he has helped raise funds for our local children's hospital; and he has taken robotics and programming courses for kids with autism. He has authored a book about his experience with spine surgery, and he has spread joy in the world just by being his loving, brilliant self. Our son is living his best life, and each opportunity has allowed our entire family to feel like part of a bigger community.

I move forward in my life always thinking of my sister and setting the bar high for what I believe my son can achieve. I work to feed his interests and help him discover his own passions. I make sure he feels like he belongs in the disabilities community so he won't have to experience loneliness on his journey. By having a vision for my child's life, and finding people who believed that vision too, I was able to find support and partnership. The initial step from isolation to involvement has led me down a path I never expected at the beginning of this journey, but my life feels fuller and richer than I could have imagined.

As you look for spaces to connect, reach out to organizations that serve people with disabilities and their families. This is a great way to find friends and mentors who can help you find resources, connect with others and think through problems that arise.

• • • • •

STEPS TO OVERCOME LONELINESS

Find your allies

Online communities, your church or spiritual community, and local support groups can connect you to other families that understand the journey you are on. Don't be afraid to explore these options, and don't give up if you don't find the right fit immediately. Not every group or connection will be the best one for you.

Your doctor, and even your child's doctors or social workers, might be able to connect you with other families like yours. It's okay to ask.

Connect to learn

Follow adults with disabilities on social media to learn about the issues that affect their lives. The experiences they share and discussions they have can help parents learn more about disability issues. You can also follow organizations that serve families of children with disabilities to broaden your knowledge.

Consider forming a virtual disability studies book club or other virtual learning opportunities. You can find autism training programs for families, modules on different medical and mental health issues, and webinars or talks related to disabilities and parenting.

Focus on the daily miracles

As parents, we should always have a vision of what our child's future can be — big, beautiful goals that defy what any professional has told us about a diagnosis or prognosis. But we should also remember to find the miracles in today.

Find someone to celebrate the daily miracles with you, whether it's a teacher or therapist, or even parents in an online community. Knowing someone cares about you and your child can help dissolve feelings of loneliness.

Tap into your sense of purpose

Having a child with a disabilities makes you have to put on your big girls pants, sometimes many times in a day. Our children need us to step up to the challenges and be advocates for them. That can be a great way to focus our energy on a new purpose.

We can overcome loneliness by sharing our knowledge, working on solutions for other families, and finding ways to make the path easier for someone else.

Chapter 2
Love

THE EMOTION

When I hear the word **love**, the first thing that pops into my mind is the song written by Musiq SoulChild. It talks about two people who fall in love at a young age. No matter the struggles, and even as they get old, they still love each other dearly like when they first met. This kind of love gives you butterflies in your stomach and cartoony heart-shaped eyes, and it makes you feel like you are floating on a cloud. This kind of love is one of intimacy, a deep connection between two people. It involves feelings of attraction and arousal.

By contrast, the love between friends is one of sisterhood, trust, close bonds, and respect. Your sisters, by blood or by choice, are peers and supporters. Sisterly love is non-competitive and can be a foundation for building our confidence and sense of connection. If your sister circle doesn't feel like this, it's time to get a new circle.

The love between a mother and a child is different from romantic or sisterly love. This love is stronger than any other love I have experienced. The bond between mother and child is developed before birth, usually from the moment the mother knows she is expecting. The mother's dreams immediately soar high for the child, and her hope in the future is draped over that child's life even before she lays eyes on the child.

THE CHALLENGES

The love a mother has for her child involves sacrifice, patience, and selflessness. Because of the love I have for my children, I made certain sacrifices to give them the best life I could possibly give them. When people compliment me on my commitment to my children, I always say, "The children we have did not ask to be here." We ushered them into this world, and it is our duty as parents to protect them, guide them, love them and give them the tools they need to navigate this world. I have sacrificed so much for my children, and the love I have for them drives me to be the best advocate, mother, businessperson and community leader that I can be.

My story of motherly love began with my firstborn, but I experienced it differently the second time around. After 16 hours of labor, I pushed a seven pound, six ounce baby boy into this world. As I lay there, anxiously anticipating holding him, I noticed the doctors and nurses were all huddled around him. I immediately felt a rush of fear. I had heard him cry, so I knew he was breathing, but I could feel the sense of concern and urgency among the doctors and nurses in the room. I had no idea what was going on. They laid him on my chest, and immediately I had butterflies in my stomach and my heart began to beat fast. I knew at that very moment that I had fallen deeply in love.

Immediately, I saw that my new baby had one blue eye. The pediatric ophthalmologist came to my room to tell me that my son had congenital glaucoma and that they would have to perform a procedure to help relieve the pressure in his eye so he would not lose his vision. Surgery! My baby was only hours out of the womb, and I was being told he would have to endure anesthesia and a surgery. I cried and immediately began to blame myself. Did I do something wrong during my pregnancy? Was this a punishment from God? All kinds of thoughts traveled through my mind.

This was my introduction to parenting a child who has medical needs. This surgery ended up being the first of many hospitalizations and treatments as we went through the process of diagnosis for a medically complex condition. My love for my son kept me motivated and looking for solutions.

HARNESSING THE POWER OF LOVE

Love is patient

Patience is necessary when caring for your loved one with a disability, and it is necessary for your child's siblings, teachers, therapists, doctors, daycare workers, and anyone else connected to your child. As a toddler, my son was extremely impulsive. He was a "runner," which means if I opened any door, he would bolt right out it. At daycare, he had to have a one-to-one aide to make sure he would not run out of the room or the building. They also had to have signs on his classroom door to let people know that there was a child who might elope. Everyone had to close the door immediately when they went in and out of his preschool classroom.

During this time, I remember always feeling anxious, worried, and scared. My son was what I called a loose cannon – he was constantly hitting, scratching and running. He was having meltdowns on a regular basis. If it was not for the grace of God, he would have been kicked out of his daycare. I felt alone and felt that no one could understand what I was going through; there were times were I wanted to pull my hair out. But then I would look at his beautiful little face and remember that he could not control or even understand why he was behaving this way. It was in those moments that I had to remember love is patient.

I began to pay closer attention when my son had meltdowns. I noticed what activities he was doing prior to the meltdowns and discovered his pattern. He was not yet talking, and he would have meltdowns when he was trying to communicate something to me that I did not understand. I learned that my son's meltdowns were driven by a sense of being overwhelmed; he was overwhelmed because he was trying to communicate with me and could not! The realization felt like a victory. Finally, I had learned something about my son's behavior, and I felt able to help him. My love for my son helped me to be patient when he needed it.

Love is motivation

By the time my son was 18 months old, I had noticed that he was not hitting certain developmental milestones like his older brother had. He did not sit up on his own until he was nine months old. He didn't crawl until he was a year old. He didn't walk until he was 18 months old, and he was non-verbal. I knew there had to be something going on, and my love for my son made me determined to find out what it was. I contacted our pediatrician, and we began to working together to have my son assessed. Help Me Grow was a key player in receiving his initial diagnoses and helping to get him connected with the proper services.

> *By nature, I am a problem solver, but when my son was diagnosed with autism, I knew this was not some problem to be solved.*

I was no stranger to the world of mental health and disability. When I was twelve years old, my mom was diagnosed with paranoid schizophrenia. I loved my mom, but the disability took her away from me mentally. She could not provide the love and attention that I needed from my mom as a little girl, through no fault of her own. I swore that when I had kids I was going to love them and give them everything that they needed, no matter what.

By nature, I am a problem solver, but when my son was diagnosed with autism, I knew this was not some problem to be solved. Instead, I needed to focus my energy on making sure he received the proper services he needed to thrive. During this time, I was determined to educate myself on my son and his diagnosis. I read books, listened to podcasts, and surrounded myself with professionals who could help me to understand what my son was going through so I could care for him and meet his needs. Love can motivate you to be the best parent that you can be.

Love is sacrifice

At the same time my son was diagnosed with autism, he began to develop seizures. It was a very scary time in our lives. He began having seizures quite often, and he was eventually diagnosed with epilepsy. I had to make a decision to move from a suburb back to the city of Cleveland so we could be closer to my son's specialists at Rainbow Babies & Children's Hospital.

I struggled with this decision because my mom had kept me in the same school district from kindergarten to high school. I admired how she had created that stability for me as a child, and I wanted the same for my children. My oldest son was in third grade at the time, and I did not want to disrupt his routine by taking him out of his school and transferring him to a new school. I had to make a tough decision after talking it over with my oldest son's father; we decided it would be best if he stayed with his dad and remained enrolled at his current school. It was painful for me to make this decision, but I did what I felt was necessary for my children's future.

I had dreams of becoming a nurse, but I had to put those dreams on hold once we received the diagnoses of epilepsy and autism. Our schedule was filled with appointments for speech therapy, occupational therapy, physical therapy, the behavioral specialist, gastroenterologist, neurologist, and ophthalmologist. Little did I know that through this journey, I would become a nurse – just not in a traditional sense. I had to make sure that I worked jobs that offered a flexible schedule. I always made sure to let my employer know up front that I have a son with a disability and that due to his complex medical conditions, I might need time away unexpectedly. I nearly lost a job because of the many times I had to be away from work. I knew then that, going forward, a flexible work schedule was what my family and I needed.

Finding work that is flexible can be a challenge, and we usually take the jobs we can get when we need work. I am thankful that God answers prayers; the last three jobs were all flexible with my lifestyle. For me, love meant not only sacrificing my dreams and wants in order to create a better environment for my family, but also adapting my life to meet my family's needs.

REMEMBER BALANCE

It's important to remember that while we sacrifice for love, we also have to create balance. We cannot sacrifice our family's wellbeing to meet the needs of one child; the whole family system needs to remain strong. If you are spending many hours each week on therapies but neglecting your marriage, your other children or yourself, you will need to reevaluate that balance. This is something we have to look at and think about as things change in our lives and in our children's lives.

Ultimately, love is transformative. It creates new strengths in us and drives us to be our best.

PART II
Breaking Chains

Love arrives
and in its train come ecstasies
old memories of pleasure
ancient histories of pain.
Yet if we are bold,
love strikes away the chains of fear
from our souls.

Second stanza of "Touched by An Angel"
by Dr. Maya Angelou

Chapter 3
Pain

THE EMOTION

Pain is the internal alarm system that warns us that something is wrong. Pain is a four-letter word that transcends verbal communication; it can be seen in facial expressions, in a moan, tears, quiet stares. It can be felt across a continent. It can be witnessed with a last breath. I could give you the Google definition of pain, but I won't, because pain is individualized and no two individuals experience pain in the exact same way.

As parents and caregivers of individuals with disabilities, the journey of pain can start with the initial diagnosis of a disability. It did for me. My son was diagnosed at the age of two with Pervasive Developmental Disorder, a condition that falls on the autism spectrum. The neurologist laid out all the things that Matthew would never do or become, from present into adulthood, all within one sentence. I sat there in shock and disbelief. I started to experience profound grief that felt like the grief I had experienced when my two other sons were born sleeping. My brain could not process the grief because my son was here, alive and breathing, looking straight into my eyes. I left the doctor's office feeling numbed by the devastating prognosis.

THE CHALLENGES

I'm sure every parent or caregiver has their own unique story of receiving that initial diagnosis and the pain that followed, but no one tells us how to process this pain. I learned years later of a term called *chronic grief*. Throughout my parenting journey, chronic grief has visited me in waves, triggered by milestones that I know my son will never achieve, like getting married, having a family, and more. This sense of loss is painful; parents and caregivers have to grieve their initial plans and dreams, and that grief and pain can happen many times over. Reading about chronic grief helped me identify what I was feeling and why. Having this information validated my feelings, and I hope it will do the same for you.

It's important for us to receive validation for what we are feeling, especially as African American women. Many times, we are expected to be all things to all people. We are expected to never let them see us sweat. The persona of being a strong black woman, especially in the role of a parent of an individual with a disability, is just that – a persona. A persona is a perception, but it's not real. No one is strong all the time; finding that perfect balance is liberating, and it allows us to express our pain without being consumed by it. Pain can be the very tool that God uses to bring liberation.

Many times, we choose to run and hide from pain, but pain gets our attention when nothing else can. I'm notorious for allowing my busy schedule as a caregiver to take front and center of my life. My day is composed of one huge checklist of activities and responsibilities. If I accomplish everything on that checklist for the day, then all is well. That changed for me one day. I was driving and developed shortness of breath and pain shooting down my arm. I was certain I was experiencing a heart attack. It was an absolutely frightening experience. When I was transported to the hospital and was in the emergency room, that pain got my attention in a way that I could no longer ignore.

> As African American women, we often shy away from professional mental health support, and this is something that needs to change in our community.

My body and my emotions took control that day, and I was introduced to my first full blown panic attack. I opened up and shared my experience with other parents, and I was amazed to discover that it was a common occurrence among parents and caregivers of individuals with disabilities. Post-traumatic stress disorder (PTSD) can present itself in the form of panic attacks. In the support groups that I have attended, this topic is not always discussed openly or even addressed as a major concern for families. It appears that parents and caregivers usually suffer in silence without getting the needed resources, information, and support.

As African American women, we often shy away from professional mental health support, and this is something that needs to change in our community. We have a right to mental wellness, just like everyone else. There are many tools available to help us deal with the pain and grief we experience, and we need to be willing to try these tools and see which ones work best in our lives. Our needs change over time, and we often have to reevaluate the supports we need to function – in the same way we advocate doing for the individual we are caring for.

As a caregiver, there must be balance. I found out how much I was out of balance when a counselor asked me, “If you were on an airplane and the emergency mask dropped down, would you put the mask on your son or yourself first?”

I replied, “My son, of course.”

She asked, “After you collapse, who will then take care of him?” I received this as one of the most important revelations of my life, which helped change my perception of how I perform my role as a caregiver. I had to pay attention to my own needs in order to meet the task of caring for my son.

We hear about self-care as caregivers, and we often approach it in a superficial way. We might plan spa days, weekend retreats, girls’ nights out, date nights and other periodic activities in our attempts to “do” self-care. We have to understand that self-care is not a list of scheduled activities that turn into additional obligations and to-do lists. Instead, self-care has to become a part of our daily lives, and it has to be internal as well as external. Self-care encompasses your mind, body, soul, and spirit and has to be integrated into your daily activities. True self-care is a way to help ourselves heal from pain, one day at a time.

• • • • •

LESSONS IN HEALING

Develop your self-care plan of action

It's not unusual to feel overwhelmed, but it's not healthy to remain overwhelmed. We have to put tools in place to deal with our emotions and function at our best. Parents and caregivers need to develop a plan of action that we can follow for self-care; this is as important as any advocacy or plan of action you put in place for your child. When we see our children struggling, we call in the cavalry and create solutions. We have to love ourselves enough to do the same for our own wellness. Having a self-care plan of action will not only benefit you, it will indirectly benefit the one you are advocating for, because what affects you will also affect them. Your self-care plan of action is a set of goals, tools and objectives to promote the best outcomes for you to be physically, mentally, and spiritually complete.

Your self-care plan of action should be developed with your team of supports; it's not something you should do alone. The goal is to take items off your plate, not to introduce more – you're doing more than enough already. Supports within the community like the church, support groups, professional counseling, primary care physicians and more can help you put your plan into action. A holistic self-care plan of action should focus on you as a whole person: your body, mind, soul, and spirit. As life brings change and new challenges, your plan will have to adapt to fit your life and your workload. You may need more supports to thrive through more difficult times.

Pain takes on different forms – physical, emotional and spiritual. It is not wise to ignore pain in any of these areas. As parents and caregivers, we can become accustomed to feeling overly tired and operating on fumes. Anxiety and stress, combined with lack of sleep, can be a toxic combination. It is absolutely necessary for parents and caregivers to get annual physical exams and well checkups and to make sure we are practicing preventive health. We also have to include adequate sleep in our plan and find the support we need to make that happen.

Manicures and massages are not a self-care substitute for basic healthcare. Please don't ignore that physical pain or use the excuse "I've just been too busy." If you are too busy to practice preventive health, you are ignoring the very basics of self-care, and no number of girls' nights out can make up for that.

Make yourself a sticky note of this self-care checklist:

- ☐ Well visits
- ☐ Healthy eating habits
- ☐ Exercise
- ☐ Good sleep and rest habits
- ☐ Quiet time
- ☐ Social support

These tools, in balance with each other, are the foundation of healthy self-care.

Healing from emotional pain

Emotional pain can also have a direct correlation to your physical health. It is amazing how God made our bodies. I shared earlier how I was introduced to my first panic attack. What I did after that episode was life changing; I made the decision to get professional counseling. Counseling became my lifeline for dealing with emotions I had ignored and hidden deep inside.

Through counseling, I was able to see that the way I thought about being a parent and caregiver was affecting me emotionally. I had established in my thinking that as long as I was able to complete my daily checklist of goals and responsibilities, I was fine. I had no idea that, emotionally, I was crumbling into tiny pieces. Within the first year of counseling, I stopped having panic attacks. Although I still experience anxiety, I no longer ignore it. Instead, I use the tools counseling has given me to manage anxiety. Counseling has become a part of my self-care plan of action, and it has improved my quality of life and strengthened me spiritually.

> There is a buffet of support that is available to parents and caregivers, so no one should starve from lack of support.

Culturally, as African Americans, we often view professional counseling in a negative light, which is why counseling is not traditionally a method of support that Black families embrace. It is important that we embrace wellness in all forms, including emotional. Health insurance plans are required to have a mental health component that will allow counseling with little or no co-pay, which helps to make sure counseling is affordable for everyone. You can find a counselor to fit your individual needs, too. My preference has been Black women counselors who understand my cultural background as well as my other needs.

Let me encourage you that if you need support, there is a counseling option for you, whether it's individual counseling, group counseling or support groups. There is a buffet of support that is available to parents and caregivers, so no one should starve from lack of support. But like any buffet, it is your decision to partake.

Healing from spiritual pain

I am a faith-led woman, so the best counselor for me was a Christian counselor. As a Christian, I gravitate to support that is spiritually based. Initially, when my son was diagnosed, I prayed consistently for God's divine healing. It was emotionally and spiritually exhausting. Eventually, God changed my heart and a new prayer emerged – I prayed that Matthew would walk in his own personal victory, in spite of the challenges he faces with autism. God has answered this new prayer. I no longer see Matthew's disability first. I see his unconditional love, his sweet character, and his big, irresistible smile.

As an African American worshipping in a traditional Black church, I did not find the information and support I needed; I must admit that it was disheartening. Our Black churches have struggled with supporting individuals with disabilities and their families. I have found that God transcends the four walls of traditional churches and has provided me spiritual support on so many levels. There are Christian-based supports for parents of individuals with disabilities. Christians will find that the Bible, through the ministry of Jesus Christ, speaks to our families with

His words of support, comfort, love and hope. There is a movement to promote change within our African American churches by providing information, training and resources that will assist them in becoming a resource to individuals with disabilities and their families within the Black community.

No matter what your faith or spiritual practice is, make it part of your self-care plan of action so it can serve to sustain and heal you.

Chapter 4
Boldness & Bravery

THE EMOTIONS

Most of the time, we don't see ourselves as courageous while we carry out the duties of parenting. I admit that I struggled at first to think of examples for this chapter because I do what I need to do for my child and I don't always see that as bravery. But every time you step out of your comfort zone to do something new and achieve a new goal, you are showing bravery.

THE CHALLENGES

I found new boldness and bravery as we went through the struggles of getting an autism diagnosis for my son. I went to two or three pediatric psychologists over several years, and they all told me Elijah was not autistic. As his mother, I knew the diagnosis of developmental delay was not all I was seeing. The doctors said his diagnosis couldn't be autism because he was able, at times, to participate in conversations and be social.

They didn't see what I saw as a parent – that he only seemed comfortable talking to adults, that his conversations were repetitive and his topics were narrow. Along with all the other things I knew about my son's behaviors and needs, I felt their conclusions were wrong. Deep down in my heart and my spirit, I knew my son had autism. I had done the research; I had done my homework. Still, I trusted what they told me because they were the experts with all the degrees and knowledge.

As we developed school supports for Elijah, we needed a formal diagnosis of autism, which meant going for a medical diagnosis again. I dreaded the process and feared that, once again, they would tell me I was wrong. On the morning of the appointment, I prayed for the courage and strength I would need to fight for my son. By the time I walked in, I felt like superwoman. I was not going to let them tell me anything different than what I knew about my child. To my surprise, the psychologist was amazing. She didn't use her degree or titles to make me feel inferior; she listened to my concerns as I explained our journey to get an autism diagnosis. I explained what I had seen over the years and why I thought autism was the right diagnosis. After a few hours of testing, she came out and confirmed with confidence that Elijah was autistic. I was elated that finally, after all these years, someone had listened to me and had seen what I'd seen. Laying my case before the doctor was a practice in bravery. Getting the autism diagnosis helped us open a world of services and resources.

• • • • •

STEPPING INTO YOUR ROLE AS AN ADVOCATE

You know your child best

Advocacy starts with the understanding that you know your child best. You will often have to stand up for their interests with people who are experts but do not know your child as well as you do. If you are fortunate, you will deal with professionals and experts who listen to you, consider your input, answer your questions and work with you on solutions.

When I first started participating in IEP meetings, I was clueless. I had no idea how the process was supposed to go. I sat and listened as they told me what Elijah needed. I nodded and smiled and followed their suggestions because they were the professionals – I thought they knew better than I did what would help him. Over the next couple of years, I learned from podcasts and from other parents that my voice was important in the process. The IEP sets the tone for my son's educational experience, and I had to be an active participant to make sure his strengths and needs were addressed.

The next year, I spoke up for the first time in an IEP meeting. I still felt nervous that they would look at me like I didn't know what I was talking about, or deny Elijah services. With my heart beating out of my chest, I told them what I wanted Elijah to work on and which goals I wanted them to implement. The team looked a little shocked as I pushed back and asked them to change some of the goals they had proposed. They had seen me be a passive participant for a couple of years, but now I was empowered to speak up. After that meeting, the team treated me differently. I was no longer a parent who sat silently and signed off on the documents – I was part of the team. I had a voice at that table, and my voice mattered.

Over time, I have learned about teambuilding and communication to help me work with professionals at school and in healthcare. Working through disagreements is a particular skill I have had to work on. There have been times when I was frustrated and angry, and my communication with these teams wasn't the greatest. Yelling and hollering will shut a meeting down fast!

> I knew if professionals didn't want to deal with me, they also might not do their best for my child.

I had to do some self-reflection on how my behavior in these moments would affect my child's outcomes. I knew if professionals didn't want to deal with me, they also might not do their best for my child. I learned from other parents about more effective ways to communicate, and I made some changes so I could be a better team member.

Trust your gut

Along with pushing through our own fears and anxieties, we often have to deal with the obstacle of how others see us. The doctors who ignored my concerns over the years were seeing Elijah through their lens as professionals, but they didn't give credibility to my knowledge about my child. They might have had biases that prevented them from listening to me or really seeing my son. Their inability to listen and collaborate meant a delay in the supports and services Elijah needed. This happens far too often and is one of the major racial disparities in autism.

We need to trust our knowledge and not assume professionals will always have the right skills or the right intentions to get the best from our children. If you are certain a diagnosis doesn't seem right, get a second opinion. If the right supports are not in place, advocate and speak up for your child's needs.

We often bear the burden of proving our children's needs for waivers, with doctors and in schools. Learning to take good notes and keep track of what is happening can help us build credibility. Having solid data, rather than just your intuition, can help you get the support your child needs. Whether you take videos, document behaviors in charts or make journal notes, be sure you have the information to show what is happening with your child.

Step up to serve others

I believe we are chosen to walk this path because we have the strength and capabilities to carry out His plan of caring for these loved ones with unique abilities. Sometimes, we lack confidence and assurance in ourselves, which makes us struggle with the task at hand. When I don't know which way to go, my relationship with the Lord helps me overcome this lack of confidence. I read and study the word, and I pray for guidance in my parenting. All of this helps me to maintain my constant connection with the Lord. I stay connected with people who encourage me and other parents on similar journeys. All of this brings me strength when I don't feel brave enough to carry out a particular task.

I am a servant at heart and I have always wanted to help and serve others. It brings joy to my heart to support other families. Still, when my church asked me to form a support group for families of people with disabilities, I wasn't so sure I could do it. I knew I had information that could help a lot of families, but I wasn't sure I was ready since I was still dealing with feelings of loneliness, isolation and fear.

In 2017, I was sharing a major milestone Elijah had in his medical care with an elder from my church. He had made it through a dental appointment successfully – no sensory meltdown – for the first time. As I shared my joy about this milestone with my church elder, the elder looked me in the eyes and said, "It's time." It was time for me to start a support group for parents, and I could feel that in my spirit. That day, she helped me develop a whole plan for the organization which became Mother 2 Mother, but even then, I wasn't sure I was the one to lead it. I had never led a support group and I didn't feel qualified.

> *Our bravery shows when we think beyond barriers and obstacles to solve a problem or reach out to others.*

Maybe you have also developed the habit of second-guessing your strength. We have to remember that our role as parent and caregiver qualifies us. We have no choice but to think outside the box as we find solutions for our child. That is a great skill to have. We are used to being outside our comfort zones, which means we have many opportunities to practice boldness. Our bravery shows when we think beyond barriers and obstacles to solve a problem or reach out to others.

PART III
Finding Strength & Purpose

We are weaned from our timidity
In the flush of love's light
we dare be brave
And suddenly we see
that love costs all we are
and will ever be.
Yet it is only love
which sets us free.

Last stanza of "Touched by An Angel"
by Dr. Maya Angelou

Chapter 5
Fear & Timidity

THE EMOTIONS

Whenever we are threatened by harm, whether imaginary or real, fear is triggered. The threat can be physical, emotional, or psychological; as long as we perceive it as a threat, then we will experience fear. Our adrenaline kicks in and our response is fight or flight. Fear is an emotion that is useful in keeping us safe in the midst of danger. We all have experienced some level of fear in our lives. Yet how we respond to ongoing fear can bring significant challenges into our lives. Ongoing fear can take on a life within itself, and everything we do or feel can revolve around it.

As a newly divorced mother of an individual with disabilities, fear became a constant in my life. I was a single African American woman having to navigate becoming the head of my household, along with the day-to-day responsibility of being the sole caregiver of my son with a disability. All of this intensified my fear. I had other ongoing fears related to living within poverty level, and my financial status challenged my ability to provide for my family and to advocate for the needs of my son. Fear at this level was not keeping me safe; it was only generating stress and anxiety.

THE CHALLENGES

When I initially meet someone and the question arises, "What kind of work do you do?" I respond that I'm an advocate for my son. But now I am an advocate for other individuals with disabilities and their families, too. I usually talk about how advocacy is a passion rather than a job, yet I rarely get the opportunity to discuss my journey and how it all began. So let me introduce you to the one responsible for this passion; his name is Matthew. I chose the name Matthew because it means a gift from God. I had mourned two pregnancies that ended with two sons born sleeping. Matthew became my miracle child, and most definitely my gift from God. My pregnancy, delivery and everything that led to bringing Matthew into the world was challenging, so I rejoiced when he was born beautiful, healthy and, most importantly, alive. I assumed that with his birth, all of the challenges I had previously faced were over. Little did I know the plans that God had for me were so different from my own.

Matthew was born in the early 90s. When Matthew was diagnosed with autism, it was during a time where little was known about this disability in the community. The roads I traveled were uncharted and sometimes terrifying. Back when Matthew was diagnosed, the occurrence of autism was about one in 10,000 individuals – he was rare. The fear that comes with that isolation was real. I felt that fear within my community, my extended family, and even my home. When we ventured out into the community, or even when we dealt with family, I felt the pain and rejection of stares and unkind comments. I felt like I needed to isolate myself from the world. The fear of rejection was as bad as the rejection itself, and it had a grip on me.

Experiencing any level of fear is a natural component of parenting an individual with disabilities. There are so many unknowns and challenges parents face, including obtaining services and home supports, navigating school, adult services and so much more. These long-term fears can become problematic, leaving us stuck in fight or flight mode, which is unhealthy emotionally and physically. Fear and danger are different. Danger is an immediate threat, like a lion sitting in the room with you. Fear that has gotten out of control can make you feel like there's immediate danger, even when there's no lion around. Feeling fear when there are no new dangers is something we need to address.

> The solution is not removing your fears – it's replacing them.

I could say "don't be afraid," as if it was that simple. I won't though, because any parent or caregiver of an individual with disabilities already knows the word "simple" is not in our vocabulary. What I will say is that while fear is real, it can be conquered. The solution is not removing your fears – it's replacing them.

On my journey of replacing my fears, I started to embrace my foundational faith in God and began to explore ways to become more informed. I felt less fearful when I learned more about my son's disability and how to get the help and services he needed. All the energy that I had directed toward responding to that long-term fear was able to be redirected.

THE POWER OF YOUR VOICE

Establishing relationships with other parents of individuals with disabilities helped me step out of my fears. Those connections brought me support, vital information and so many answers to questions that I had silently struggled with for so long. Fear was gradually being replaced with trusting relationships with professionals and parents. There were people I could talk to about my concerns before they grew into enormous fears. For me, fear became more manageable when I had access to information and resources, and when I felt able to make informed decisions. Even after gaining new knowledge, I had to learn how to apply it to the unique needs of my son. Someone once said, "Knowledge is power." This is absolutely true. Gaining knowledge was a marathon, not a sprint, but the farther along I went, the less afraid I was.

I have a vivid memory of my very first IEP meeting for my son with our local school district. I sat in the meeting surrounded by professionals who had never met us before, as they went over evaluations and information that I could barely understand. They threw around words that felt like a foreign language to me, and I felt lost – and afraid that I was out of my depth. I was told at the meeting that the consensus was that Matthew was not going to attend a school within the district. I was informed that he would be placed out-of-district and that I could choose from a list of three schools they thought would work for him.

I remember saying, "I would like my son to attend the school district in which we live." I was told in the form of a rebuke that they had nothing for him. Even though I felt fearful and intimidated, I found my voice. "Make something, because he's coming." The energy in the room shifted.

In that meeting, I also requested an aide for Matthew and was immediately told that our district didn't provide aides. Matthew took care of that predicament within a few weeks of attending school. He climbed out of a window at school after they put him in a time out and left him unattended, and no one could find him. The school didn't share that information with me immediately; all I was told when I picked him up that day was that Matthew had been assigned an aide.

This was the first major step in becoming an effective advocate for Matthew. Even though fear was still present during that IEP meeting, that fear did not control me. I was fighting for Matthew, and I pushed aside my fear to make sure he had what he needed. The resources, support, and information I had gathered from parents and professionals had given me the tools I needed to make an informed decision for my son. Fear was no longer in control.

> Remember, the information you learn outside of your community travels back with you when you return.

In my early years of learning to be an advocate, I had to become accustomed to stepping out of my comfort zone. Most of the people from whom I learned important information and tools about advocacy were not people of color. I found significant cultural differences in those associations, but I also found a wealth of knowledge. In spite of our differences, we always had one thing in common – we were advocating for someone we loved. Some of those interactions developed into meaningful relationships, which have become lifelong.

Stepping out of your comfort zone can be frightening. Attending meetings and trainings where you are the only person of color can be intimidating. If you can redirect that fear and those feelings of intimidation into your vision of achieving the goals and outcomes that you desire for your individual with disabilities, you will see that it is time well invested in the future of the one you advocate for.

Remember, the information you learn outside of your community travels back with you when your return. By growing your knowledge, you impact not just your own life, but the lives of other parents within the community that you share it with. I started my nonprofit REACH Services with this same mission in mind – to share and bring information and support to underserved individuals and people of color.

BECOMING A TRAILBLAZER

Don't let fear or intimidation influence your ability to advocate for your individual. You are the only constant in your individual's life; everyone else is a revolving door. No matter how many degrees a professional may have behind their name, no one will ever know your individual like you. Professionals can become obsessed with diagnoses and labels, but parents are more focused on addressing the present needs and building on the strengths of their individual with disabilities.

For that reason, making informed decisions and being able to prioritize what the needs are of our individual with disabilities are vital skills for parents and caregivers. The more educated you are about your individual's disability, and the more you understand their needs and strengths, the better you will become with making informed decisions. Sometimes it's up to the parent or caregiver to make others aware of strengths, when they can only see challenges.

> *Your individual has the right to be heard, respected, and given the same opportunity as anyone else to live a happy and productive life.*

Knowledge gives advocates the power to use their voice. Knowledge, combined with passion and the love for the individual you are advocating for, drives out fear. Sometimes parents feel what they have to say is not important, but remember, many times we are speaking for an individual who cannot speak for themselves. They are depending on you to speak on their behalf and validate them as an individual with rights, feelings, and self-worth, not just another case in a file or client that needs services. Your individual has the right to be heard, respected, and given the same opportunity as anyone else to live a happy and productive life. There is power in spoken words, and I've always had more regrets about what I didn't say. Those are the missed opportunities that never present themselves again.

When you are preparing for an IEP or ISP meeting, try connecting with other parents. This gives you an opportunity to share your ideas or concerns with other parents just to get insight or feedback. It allows you to practice using your voice in a safe space and get suggestions or ideas. This helps you to manage fear and feel confident when the opportunity arises to share your ideas or concerns. You can also request the topic of discussion in advance of the meeting and review it yourself or with others. This will allow you to make notes or jot down talking points before the meeting. These actions will allow you to be more prepared for the meeting and allow you to feel more relaxed.

• • • • •

OVERCOMING FEAR

Step outside your comfort zone

If you live in a community where you cannot access the information that you need to become an effective advocate, there are statewide and national organizations that can help. They provide training and workshops for parents and caregivers. Joining a parent support group is always an effective way to get access to the trainings and workshops that are available to you. Stepping out of your comfort zone and overcoming fear will keep you informed and updated on existing and new resources, within and outside your immediate community.

Stepping outside your comfort zone and traveling down a path less traveled will open the door to resources and information.

These are the first steps in becoming an effective advocate. They lay foundational groundwork and will give you the tools to make informed decisions for your individual with disabilities.

Make informed decisions

Making informed decisions for your individual with disabilities will involve obtaining knowledge, information and resources, then personalizing it to meet their individual needs. All of these things in your arsenal as an advocate will help you to manage those moments when you are fearful. There is a chain of command in making informed decisions: on top are the needs of the individual; next, the parent or caregiver who is informed about the needs of the individual and utilizing the information, education and supports obtained; then the IEP or ISP team. When the chain of command is working in perfect order, the person at the top is always the beneficiary.

An advocate is someone who is forever learning. There are always changes going on in the disability community. If we don't make ourselves available to this information, we find ourselves unable to make informed choices that will best serve the individual we are advocating for. Making informed decisions is composed of these things: knowledge, information, resources and knowing the needs of the individual you are advocating for. Knowing how to use these things in a plan of action through an IEP or an ISP is the recipe for effective advocacy.

Use your voice, find your power.

Finding your voice as an advocate will give you the opportunity to break through glass ceilings for your individual with disabilities. You will start developing characteristics of a leader and not a follower. Don't be surprised when other parents come to you for information, education, and support. The fear that you struggled with before will be replaced by a sense of purpose. There is power, passion and purpose in finding your voice.

Finding your voice does not mean you will have the answers to all the questions; it only means you will use your voice to ask all the questions that need to be answered so you will have the ability to make informed decisions. No longer will you quietly sit in a meeting and allow individuals to discuss information about your individual and without making sure you understand that information. No longer will you sign documents that are not clear to you or that don't meet the needs of your individual. No longer will you enter these spaces without seeking information or support. Finding your voice will replace fear with assertiveness, and assertiveness will lead to you becoming an effective and powerful advocate.

Chapter 6
Freedom

THE EMOTION

Let's talk about freedom. Take a moment and say that word to yourself. Freedom.

Think about what freedom feels like to you. Does it feel like floating on your back in a lake on a sunny day? Does it feel like marching or voting? How does the word freedom **feel**? To me, the word freedom feels like running with the wind on my skin, loving with an open heart and no walls, feeling life move through me.

Freedom isn't usually the first word people think of when they think about parenting, especially not parenting children with disabilities. We often think of parenting as an obligation, a duty, or a job. We treat parenting as a series of tasks we have to accomplish, an infinite to-do list – no floating on a lake or running in the wind. At first glance, nothing about parenting resembles freedom at all. But let's examine freedom a little more deeply.

The definition of freedom (according to Google) is "the power or right to act, speak, or think as one wants without hindrance or restraint." So freedom is, first and foremost, about power.

We might feel powerless at times in our parenting journey, when new diagnoses or behaviors blindside us or our plans and solutions fail. We can feel powerless when we deal with teachers, doctors and others who have decision-making power over our children's lives. We can feel small, insignificant, and almost invisible when the challenges are stacked high and our energy level is on low. But freedom is about finding our power.

THE CHALLENGES

Finding your power sounds cute, but how do you actually do it? Power has so many definitions. Knowledge is power. Information is power. Strength is power. Silence is power. We might have to use any or all of these types of power at some point. Sometimes, power is about knowing your choices. Sometimes it's about knowing who can help you achieve a goal. At times, emotion is power, and showing our passion and intensity can communicate that power. At other times, it's more powerful to be silent and observe. However we exercise our power, the act of exercising that power is freedom. One freedom we can find in parenting is choosing the actions that will give us the best results.

> We don't have to wield our knowledge like a weapon. The conversation is different when they know you are well informed.

Freedom is also about knowing and exercising your rights: how you should be treated, what you should receive, what you should expect, and what you should demand. As parents of children with disabilities, we have to know our children's rights, too. There are laws that protect their care and education, and knowing those laws makes us very powerful. Knowing your child's rights isn't about threatening to sue someone every time things don't go our way. Instead, it's a way to make sure that those rights are protected from the very start of a conversation.

I am fortunate to have a teaching background, which comes in handy when we're advocating for our son at school. My husband, who has a doctorate in education and used to be an intervention specialist, is a great partner because we both have a firm understanding of our son's rights in school and what should be done to accommodate his needs. We don't have to wield our knowledge like a weapon. The conversation is different when they know you are well informed.

The fact that we have this knowledge base means the schools start with the understanding that we expect our son's rights to be respected, no matter what. Ideally, every family would be treated equally, but that's not the reality. Those who enter with more information and knowledge tend to leave with better results. It is our responsibility as parents to build our knowledge so we can better advocate for our children's success in systems that don't always do right by them.

Freedom is about acting, thinking and speaking. Freedom is not a spectator sport. To feel freedom as parents, we have to **do** something. That freedom isn't just handed to us; we earn it by standing up, thinking deeply about solutions, and speaking out. We gain skills, and that gives us more freedom. We learn, and again we gain more freedom. Our growth is the price we pay for freedom. As they say, freedom ain't free.

NO HOLDING BACK

I realized the value of freedom with one of my son's medical specialists. We had worked together for over a year managing a complex medical issue that was life threatening. Eventually, I noticed that he leaned on my knowledge more and seemed more at ease in my son's appointments. Instead of telling me what our plan of action would be, the doctor started asking me what I wanted. And when I told him, he would write out the orders word for word. Through my actions as a parent and my involvement, I had earned the trust of this specialist in managing our son's care, to the point where the doctor took my word as law. That created a new level of freedom for me as a co-director of our son's care.

Freedom is about not being hindered or restrained. I've felt hindered many times in my parenting journey. My son has spent a lot of time in hospitals over the years, and I spent a lot of energy "presenting" – trying to make sure the doctors and nurses saw me as an involved parent so they would work hard to give our son the best care. It was absolutely exhausting to be in the middle of a medical crisis and still worry about how I was seen by these strangers. There were times when I felt like the knowledge I brought about my son's needs wasn't taken seriously, and times when I felt like I was being silenced. I felt hindered from being the best advocate I could be because the people I was dealing with, as well as my own beliefs sometimes, were holding me back.

Once, when my son was an infant, I went to his doctor and asked about different ways to feed him. He has a feeding tube, and I wanted to blend up real food instead of using a canned formula. The doctor and dietician looked really concerned about how safe it was for me to do that. They refused to write the medical order that would allow my son's home care nurses to feed him a homemade diet. When I asked what their safety concerns were, the dietician told me she was concerned that my kitchen might not be clean enough to avoid contaminating his food.

I felt that my desire to give my child real food was completely silenced by her obvious stereotyping and racism. The medical team made a decision that restrained my ability to decide for my son what was best for him. They didn't seem to get that I wasn't asking for permission; I was asking for support and a doctor's order.

I left that appointment disappointed but determined. I remembered that without his disability, my son wouldn't need special permission and could eat whatever I decided to feed him. I found a doctor who believed in real food the way I did, and we were able to get the doctor's order that would allow our in-home nurses to feed our son the homemade formula. Now nine years old, our son has been on a blenderized diet for the past seven years, and he is healthy and thriving. In this situation, I had to shed the restraints put on me by his doctors so I could have the freedom to make the decision I felt was best.

Another freedom I have felt as a parent is the freedom to share our experiences. Through my involvement with different organizations, I have had the opportunity to share with others and help them along the way. I served on my county's Board of Developmental Disabilities, and I volunteered as a mentor at our local pediatric hospital. I was a paid parent mentor for our local school district, which gave me a chance to meet other moms and help them with resources and strategies to get the best from school. Years later, I serve on several national committees and boards in healthcare and education. Over time, I even transitioned my career in communications to advocate for young children, and my nonprofit allows me to use my academic background to train families on advocacy skills. My parenting experience has made me feel free to explore new paths that I wouldn't have ordinarily taken.

> Our power, our voice, our strength is in realizing that freedom is still ours for the taking. And once we find our freedom, we share it with our children and our communities.

I know the ins and outs of our experience well enough to connect it to the bigger issues in our world, and that offers me lots of freedom. I speak freely now, knowing that our experience is valuable and no one knows it better than I do. I think more broadly, knowing our lives and challenges are related to the lives and challenges of families like ours. I am part of a global community of parents raising children with disabilities, and I am proud of the strength those numbers represent. We are powerful together, and we can act together to solve problems. That is another form of freedom.

As parents, we have to remember our power and our freedom. We can't forget what it feels like to be free. Freedom is possible, no matter what challenges we face. Our power, our voice, and our strength come from realizing that freedom is still ours for the taking – and once we find our freedom, we share it with our children and our communities.

. . . . .

GRABBING YOUR FREEDOM

Don't forget who you are

Sometimes the work of being a parent leaves us feeling disconnected from who we were before. It's important to connect with friends, loved ones and activities that bring you joy – and share this with your child. If you love painting, paint together. If you love nature, go on walks together. Remember what makes you feel free, and create time to do it.

Burnout is real, and it can really affect the quality of our parenting if we are depleted and have nothing left to give. As the parent of a child with a disability, you hear the term "self-care" thrown around a lot. It took me years to figure out what self-care meant, beyond manicures and massages. Self-care is really about filling your cup before it gets empty, finding joy and pleasure each day to protect yourself from burnout.

Put together a list of activities that make you feel free and at peace. Your list could include writing, reading, yoga, walking, cuddling and watching a movie with your partner, or playing games with your child. This list can become your daily guide to self-care, and you can choose at least one activity to do each day. Even when it feels like you don't have much spare time, 10 minutes of an activity that really feeds your soul can help you endure the challenges of the day. Steal those minutes like you're taking back your freedom.

Know your rights

When you know the laws, expectations and rules, you can command the conversation and guide others toward the goals you have for your child. Make it a point to learn how your state handles issues with special education. Read about ableism and how it affects the way we think and talk about disability. If your child has a specific diagnosis, learn everything you can about it. Write down questions and participate in the conversations about your child's needs. You will feel much more confident when you are armed with knowledge, and you will see how that changes the way people respond to you.

Find ways to use your voice

Beyond going to the mat for your own child, you will meet many other families who are dealing with difficulties as they learn how to navigate parenting a child with a disability. Local and national organizations often have parent groups so parents can offer feedback and help serve the community. Diagnosis specific organizations like The Up Side of Downs and Muscular Dystrophy Association, among many, many others, have ways for families to get involved in their work. Learn to tell your story and find freedom in knowing that your voice, your experience, is valued.

Chapter 7
Moving Forward

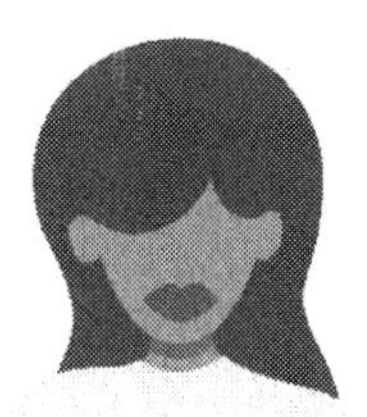  

NAVIGATING THE EMOTIONS

We've taken a journey together through the emotions that fuel our lives and guide our purpose as moms of children with disabilities. No matter what emotions or challenges we deal with, our love for our children calls on us to do more and be more so we can help our children reach their potential. We are capable and gifted. When given the choice to fold and give up, or move forward and press on, we choose to go forward. The community your child has brought you into will motivate and inspire your life. Don't take this blessing for granted.

When we started writing this book, we knew exactly how we wanted you to feel when you finished it. We wanted you to feel confident and have comfort that you could do the work of parenting and advocacy while also enjoying the joys of parenting your unique child. We wanted you to feel like you had new knowledge or skills and feel empowered to use them. We wanted you to feel like you learned something valuable and that you wouldn't feel overwhelmed or intimidated about the road ahead. Most of all, we wanted you to feel inspired to think bigger – about your life and your child's.

THE CHALLENGES

Your experiences make you part of a community, a sisterhood. Most of us didn't join this sisterhood by choice, but we are here, supporting one another and giving our children the best of ourselves, because love calls us to do that.

We can't forget the importance of community for our children either. Our children are part of the larger disabilities community—a community with its own civil rights history and oppressions, but also its own heroes and icons. Disability rights heroes should be our heroes too, because they paved the way for our children's rights and for our advocacy. We can teach our children not be feel ashamed of disability; we can teach them that they are perfect and amazing and unique.

• • • • •

BUILDING A COMMUNITY AROUND YOUR CHILD WITH DISABILITIES

Learn the history and get involved

Learn more about disability rights and disability rights history. Your child is part of this history, and understanding it is as important for our families as Black History.

Get involved in the disabilities community and local organizations that support families and make sure your child knows other people with disabilities. The disabilities community is diverse, and making sure the treatment of people with disabilities improves can begin with us. Promote positive images and positive interactions in the disabilities community.

Breaking barriers

Allow your child to explore talents—whether they participate in programs with children who don't have disabilities or join adaptive programs.

Don't be afraid to break barriers. Just because a thing hasn't been done, doesn't mean it can't be. If your child has a passion for a sport, let them play. If they love music, let them find ways to make music. Help your child find their own joy and purpose, and their own sense of community. This can be a great support to your entire family.

The Sisterhood

As you move forward in your journey, know that your success is important – to you, to your child, to your family, and to your community. We are sisters in this journey, and we are creating a world for our children, together. Our combined knowledge and understanding grows when we share and work together. Connection with others is something we all need on this journey.

We dare to meet the challenges and thrive. **We dare be brave.**

Join the discussion on Facebook.
Search: We Dare Be Brave.

About the Authors

Salina Miller, a recipient of the National Nurses Coalition's Unsung Heroes Award, is a visionary, a trailblazer, a philanthropist and the epitome of devotion. Salina's passion for service emerged with the birth of her son Elijah, who has multiple diagnoses, including autism. Her love for family and fervent desire to positively impact others' lives and advocate for individuals with special needs and their parents inspired her to create the service organization Mother 2 Mother in 2017 and dedicate her life to bringing education, empowerment and awareness to communities while providing support to special needs families.

Salina is proud to serve as a parent representative on Ohio's State Support Team III and as a member of the University Hospitals Rainbow Babies & Children's Hospital's Patient and Family Partnership Council. She has worked as a Parent Involvement Specialist for Warrensville Middle School and as a part of the Milestones Autism Resources diversity taskforce. Salina has also worked for Milestones Autism Resources as the Diversity, Equity and Inclusion Coordinator, moderating their Straight from the Source parent and self-advocate panels and facilitating educational training for police officers on how to safely interact with individuals with autism.

Learn more about the Mother 2 Mother parent community at **mother2mother.info**, and follow the community on social media **@mother2mother32**.

Patricia Parker has led her life by her favorite scripture Psalm 34:7, “Delight thyself also in the Lord, and He will give you the desires of your heart.” As an advocate and founder of Resource, Education and Community Help Services, Inc. (REACH) in Cleveland, Ohio, Patricia is a resounding voice for individuals with disabilities and their families. She earned her associate's degree in Liberal Arts from Cuyahoga Community College in addition to a bachelor's degree in Nonprofit Administration from Cleveland State University. She has written the nonfiction book, *S.I.N.G.L.E. – Let God Define You, Not Your Status*, available on Amazon.com and from Quiet Time Inspirational Books at **www.quiettime.shop**. Patricia's blogs include “Forgotten Members of the Body of Christ”, “The Disability Friendly Church” and “Highway and Hedges.”

Patricia resides in Ohio and is a divorced mother of two adult sons. Her oldest son has autism and epilepsy and has been a tremendous source of hope, strength, and inspiration in her life. Her hobbies include reading and attending theatrical plays.

Follow Patricia Parker on social media **@2quiettime**.

Charisse (Nikki) Montgomery is a patient advocate, educational psychologist and communications expert. The parent of a child with complex health needs and autism, she is passionate about improving outcomes for children and helping families advocate successfully. A former educator, her research in educational psychology focuses on informing and empowering parents of children with disabilities. Nikki serves on the Board of Directors at University Hospitals Rainbow Babies & Children's Hospital, along with many other leadership roles for disability rights, healthcare and education policy, and equity. Nikki is the executive director of Madvocator Educational and Healthcare Advocacy Training, a 501(c)(3) nonprofit. Learn more at **madvocator.org**, or follow Nikki on social media **@madvocator**.

Other titles by Charisse N. Montgomery, available from Amazon and the Super Safe Kids website. Download free resources and find books for medically complex kids at **www.supersafekidsbooks.com**. Follow the series on social media **@supersafekids**.

- *Central Line Safety for Kids*
- *Feeding Tube Safety for Kids*
- *Home Care CEO: A Parent's Guide to Managing In-Home Pediatric Nursing*
- *Hospital Safety for Kids*
- *Power Wheelchair Safety for Kids*
- *The Spine Surgery Book for Kids*
- *Tracheostomy Safety for Kids*

. . . . .

No matter what emotions or challenges
we deal with, our love for our children
calls on us to do more and be more,
so we can help our children
reach their potential.

. . . . .

Made in the USA
Middletown, DE
24 September 2022

10710957R00046